Interior Designing Mood Board Journal

Visual Presentation Of Interior Design Images, Text, And Samples (Portrait)

VIRGINIA I SMITH

VIRYABO'S
CREATIONS
INTERIOR DESIGNER

Thank you for your purchase

We hope you enjoy using this interior design workbook. If there is anything you feel may be great to add (or remove), please don't hesitate to leave a comment or a review. **Shop** our other interior design-related workbooks and activity books, sketchbooks, planners, journals, and business books created specifically for interior designers and students of interior design: https://www.amazon.com/-/e/B07ZPHJD8R

OUR RELATED BOOKS ON KDP

ASIN: B08KH3R53Q

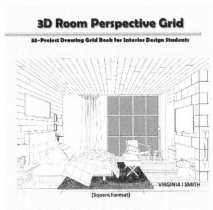

ASIN: B0BRDJYRFY

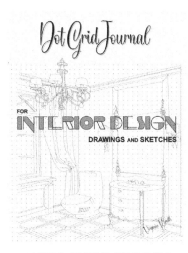

ASIN: B08BG5R36Y

ASIN: B09S64XXHS

ASIN: B08R23ZQGF

ASIN: B08CPJJG1M

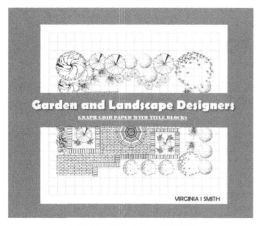

ASIN: B0C1JJTS9F

ASIN: B0B7Q3DXFW

ASIN: B09P217CT1

ASIN: B08F6CGC5M

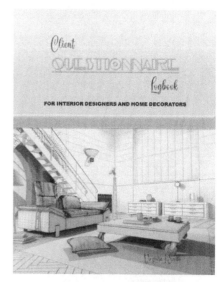

ASIN: B092H9V4YG

ASIN: B08FRVBNN1

ASIN: B0BF2XBCMG

This book belongs to

Contact:

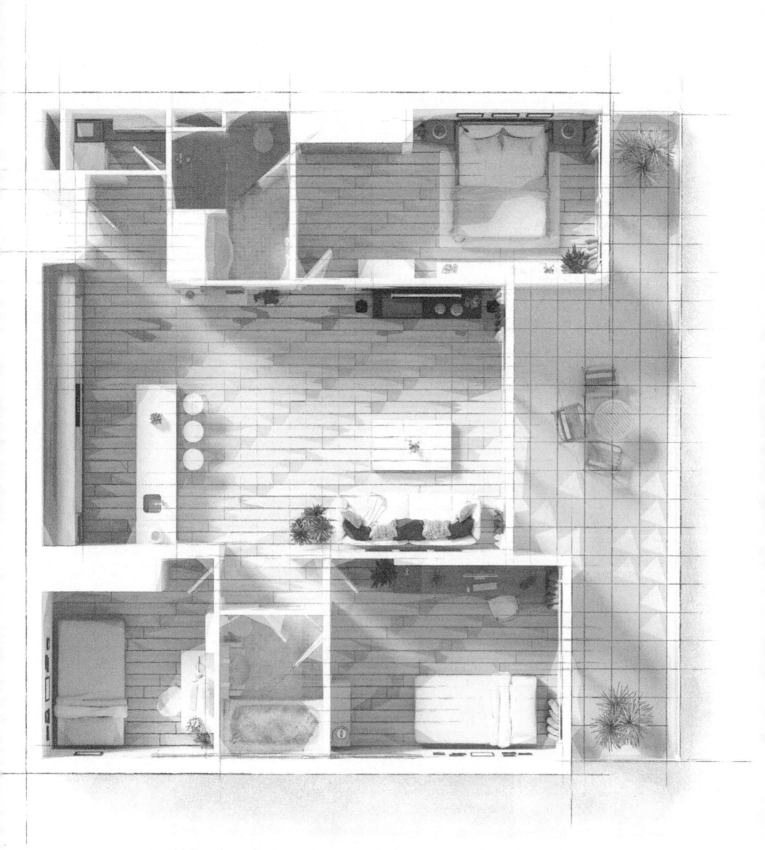

DATE

REF #

CLIENT

EMAIL

PHONE

PROJECT
TITLE

THEME

STYLE

ROOM/AREA/SPACE

AREA/SIZE/VOLUME

ADDITIONAL
INFORMATION

PROJECT BRIEF

PROJECT OBJECTIVE

ADDITIONAL NOTES

7

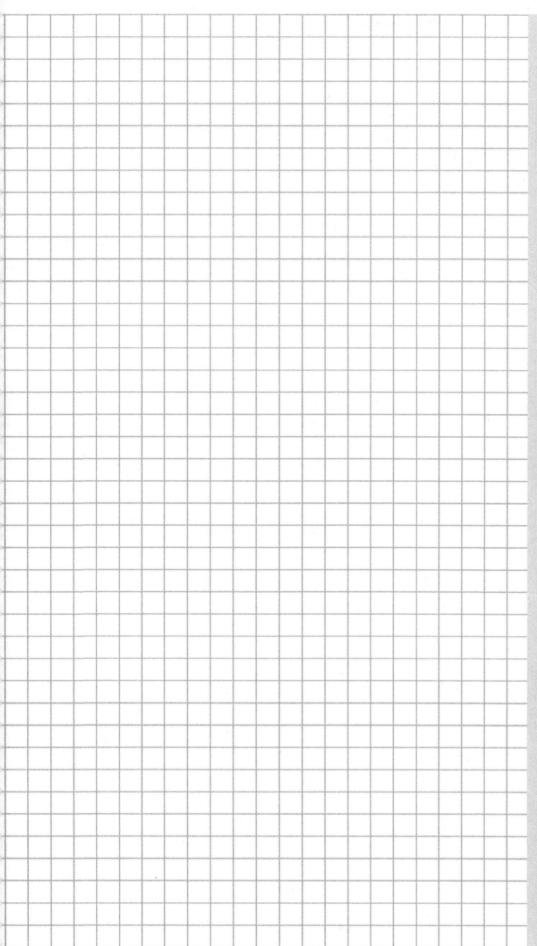

MEASUREMENTS

COLORS

TEXTURES

13

DATE

CLIENT

REF #

EMAIL

PHONE

PROJECT
TITLE

THEME

STYLE

ROOM/AREA/SPACE

AREA/SIZE/VOLUME

ADDITIONAL
INFORMATION

PROJECT BRIEF

PROJECT OBJECTIVE

ADDITIONAL NOTES

MOOD PAGE

MEASUREMENTS

COLORS

TEXTURES

NOTES

NOTES

DATE

REF #

CLIENT

EMAIL

PHONE

PROJECT
TITLE

THEME

STYLE

ROOM/AREA/SPACE

AREA/SIZE/VOLUME

ADDITIONAL
INFORMATION

PROJECT BRIEF

PROJECT OBJECTIVE

ADDITIONAL NOTES

MEASUREMENTS

COLORS

TEXTURES

NOTES

NOTES

DATE

REF #

CLIENT

EMAIL

PHONE

PROJECT TITLE

THEME

STYLE

ROOM/AREA/SPACE

AREA/SIZE/VOLUME

ADDITIONAL INFORMATION

PROJECT BRIEF

PROJECT OBJECTIVE

ADDITIONAL NOTES

MOOD PAGE

MEASUREMENTS

COLORS

TEXTURES

NOTES

NOTES

DATE

CLIENT

REF #

EMAIL

PHONE

PROJECT TITLE

THEME

STYLE

ROOM/AREA/SPACE

AREA/SIZE/VOLUME

ADDITIONAL INFORMATION

PROJECT BRIEF

PROJECT OBJECTIVE

ADDITIONAL NOTES

MEASUREMENTS

COLORS

TEXTURES

NOTES

NOTES

DATE

REF #

CLIENT

EMAIL

PHONE

PROJECT TITLE

THEME

STYLE

ROOM/AREA/SPACE

AREA/SIZE/VOLUME

ADDITIONAL INFORMATION

PROJECT BRIEF

PROJECT OBJECTIVE

ADDITIONAL NOTES

MOOD PAGE

MOOD PAGE

MEASUREMENTS

COLORS

TEXTURES

NOTES

NOTES

DATE

CLIENT

REF #

EMAIL

PHONE

PROJECT TITLE

THEME

STYLE

ROOM/AREA/SPACE

AREA/SIZE/VOLUME

ADDITIONAL INFORMATION

PROJECT BRIEF

PROJECT OBJECTIVE

ADDITIONAL NOTES

MEASUREMENTS

COLORS

TEXTURES

NOTES

NOTES

DATE

REF #

CLIENT

EMAIL

PHONE

PROJECT
TITLE

THEME

STYLE

ROOM/AREA/SPACE

AREA/SIZE/VOLUME

ADDITIONAL
INFORMATION

PROJECT BRIEF

PROJECT OBJECTIVE

ADDITIONAL NOTES

MEASUREMENTS

COLORS

TEXTURES

NOTES

NOTES

DATE

REF #

CLIENT

EMAIL

PHONE

PROJECT
TITLE

THEME

STYLE

ROOM/AREA/SPACE

AREA/SIZE/VOLUME

ADDITIONAL
INFORMATION

PROJECT BRIEF

PROJECT OBJECTIVE

ADDITIONAL NOTES

MOOD PAGE

MEASUREMENTS

COLORS

TEXTURES

NOTES	NOTES

DATE

REF #

CLIENT

EMAIL

PHONE

PROJECT TITLE

THEME

STYLE

ROOM/AREA/SPACE

AREA/SIZE/VOLUME

ADDITIONAL INFORMATION

PROJECT BRIEF

PROJECT OBJECTIVE

ADDITIONAL NOTES

MEASUREMENTS

COLORS

TEXTURES

NOTES

NOTES

DATE

REF #

CLIENT

EMAIL

PHONE

PROJECT TITLE

THEME

STYLE

ROOM/AREA/SPACE

AREA/SIZE/VOLUME

ADDITIONAL INFORMATION

PROJECT BRIEF

PROJECT OBJECTIVE

ADDITIONAL NOTES

MEASUREMENTS

COLORS

TEXTURES

NOTES

NOTES

DATE

CLIENT

REF #

EMAIL

PHONE

PROJECT TITLE

THEME

STYLE

ROOM/AREA/SPACE

AREA/SIZE/VOLUME

ADDITIONAL INFORMATION

PROJECT BRIEF

PROJECT OBJECTIVE

ADDITIONAL NOTES

MOOD PAGE

MEASUREMENTS

COLORS

TEXTURES

NOTES

NOTES

DATE

CLIENT

REF #

EMAIL

PHONE

PROJECT
TITLE

THEME

STYLE

ROOM/AREA/SPACE

AREA/SIZE/VOLUME

ADDITIONAL
INFORMATION

PROJECT BRIEF

PROJECT OBJECTIVE

ADDITIONAL NOTES

MOOD PAGE

MOOD PAGE

MOOD PAGE

MEASUREMENTS

COLORS

TEXTURES

NOTES

NOTES

109

DATE

CLIENT

REF #

EMAIL

PHONE

PROJECT
TITLE

THEME

STYLE

ROOM/AREA/SPACE

AREA/SIZE/VOLUME

ADDITIONAL
INFORMATION

PROJECT BRIEF

PROJECT OBJECTIVE

ADDITIONAL NOTES

NOTES

MEASUREMENTS

COLORS

TEXTURES

NOTES

NOTES

DATE			REF #	
CLIENT			EMAIL	
			PHONE	

| PROJECT TITLE | |
| THEME | | STYLE | |

| ROOM/AREA/SPACE | | | | | |
| AREA/SIZE/VOLUME | | | | | |

ADDITIONAL INFORMATION

PROJECT BRIEF

PROJECT OBJECTIVE

ADDITIONAL NOTES

MOOD PAGE

NOTES

MEASUREMENTS

COLORS

TEXTURES

NOTES

NOTES

DATE

REF #

EMAIL

CLIENT

PHONE

PROJECT
TITLE

THEME

STYLE

ROOM/AREA/SPACE

AREA/SIZE/VOLUME

ADDITIONAL
INFORMATION

PROJECT BRIEF

PROJECT OBJECTIVE

ADDITIONAL NOTES

MEASUREMENTS

COLORS

TEXTURES

NOTES

NOTES

DATE

CLIENT

REF #

EMAIL

PHONE

PROJECT TITLE

THEME

STYLE

ROOM/AREA/SPACE

AREA/SIZE/VOLUME

ADDITIONAL INFORMATION

PROJECT BRIEF

PROJECT OBJECTIVE

ADDITIONAL NOTES

MEASUREMENTS

COLORS

TEXTURES

NOTES

NOTES

DATE

REF #

CLIENT

EMAIL

PHONE

PROJECT TITLE

THEME

STYLE

ROOM/AREA/SPACE

AREA/SIZE/VOLUME

ADDITIONAL INFORMATION

PROJECT BRIEF

PROJECT OBJECTIVE

ADDITIONAL NOTES

MOOD PAGE

NOTES

MEASUREMENTS

COLORS

TEXTURES

DATE

REF #

CLIENT

EMAIL

PHONE

PROJECT TITLE

THEME

STYLE

ROOM/AREA/SPACE

AREA/SIZE/VOLUME

ADDITIONAL INFORMATION

PROJECT BRIEF

PROJECT OBJECTIVE

ADDITIONAL NOTES

MOOD PAGE

MEASUREMENTS

COLORS

TEXTURES

NOTES

NOTES

DATE		REF #	
CLIENT		EMAIL	
		PHONE	

PROJECT TITLE

THEME | | **STYLE** |

ROOM/AREA/SPACE

AREA/SIZE/VOLUME

ADDITIONAL INFORMATION

PROJECT BRIEF

PROJECT OBJECTIVE

ADDITIONAL NOTES

MOOD PAGE

MEASUREMENTS

COLORS

TEXTURES

NOTES

NOTES

DATE

CLIENT

REF #

EMAIL

PHONE

PROJECT
TITLE

THEME

STYLE

ROOM/AREA/SPACE

AREA/SIZE/VOLUME

ADDITIONAL
INFORMATION

PROJECT BRIEF

PROJECT OBJECTIVE

ADDITIONAL NOTES

MOOD PAGE

MEASUREMENTS

COLORS

TEXTURES

NOTES

NOTES

DATE		REF #	
CLIENT		EMAIL	
		PHONE	

PROJECT TITLE

THEME

STYLE

ROOM/AREA/SPACE

AREA/SIZE/VOLUME

ADDITIONAL INFORMATION

PROJECT BRIEF

PROJECT OBJECTIVE

ADDITIONAL NOTES

NOTES

MEASUREMENTS

COLORS

TEXTURES

NOTES

NOTES

DATE

CLIENT

PROJECT
TITLE

THEME

REF #

EMAIL

PHONE

STYLE

ROOM/AREA/SPACE

AREA/SIZE/VOLUME

ADDITIONAL
INFORMATION

PROJECT BRIEF

PROJECT OBJECTIVE

ADDITIONAL NOTES

MEASUREMENTS

COLORS

TEXTURES

NOTES

NOTES

DATE

REF #

CLIENT

EMAIL

PHONE

PROJECT
TITLE

THEME

STYLE

ROOM/AREA/SPACE

AREA/SIZE/VOLUME

ADDITIONAL
INFORMATION

PROJECT BRIEF

PROJECT OBJECTIVE

ADDITIONAL NOTES

MOOD PAGE

MEASUREMENTS

COLORS

TEXTURES

NOTES

NOTES

DATE

REF #

CLIENT

EMAIL

PHONE

PROJECT TITLE

THEME

STYLE

ROOM/AREA/SPACE

AREA/SIZE/VOLUME

ADDITIONAL INFORMATION

PROJECT BRIEF

PROJECT OBJECTIVE

ADDITIONAL NOTES

MOOD PAGE

MOOD PAGE

NOTES

MEASUREMENTS

COLORS

TEXTURES

NOTES

NOTES

DATE

REF #

CLIENT

EMAIL

PHONE

PROJECT
TITLE

THEME

STYLE

ROOM/AREA/SPACE

AREA/SIZE/VOLUME

ADDITIONAL
INFORMATION

PROJECT BRIEF

PROJECT OBJECTIVE

ADDITIONAL NOTES

MEASUREMENTS

COLORS

TEXTURES

NOTES

NOTES

DATE		REF #	
		EMAIL	
CLIENT		PHONE	

PROJECT TITLE

THEME | | STYLE |

ROOM/AREA/SPACE

AREA/SIZE/VOLUME

ADDITIONAL INFORMATION

PROJECT BRIEF

PROJECT OBJECTIVE

ADDITIONAL NOTES

MOOD PAGE

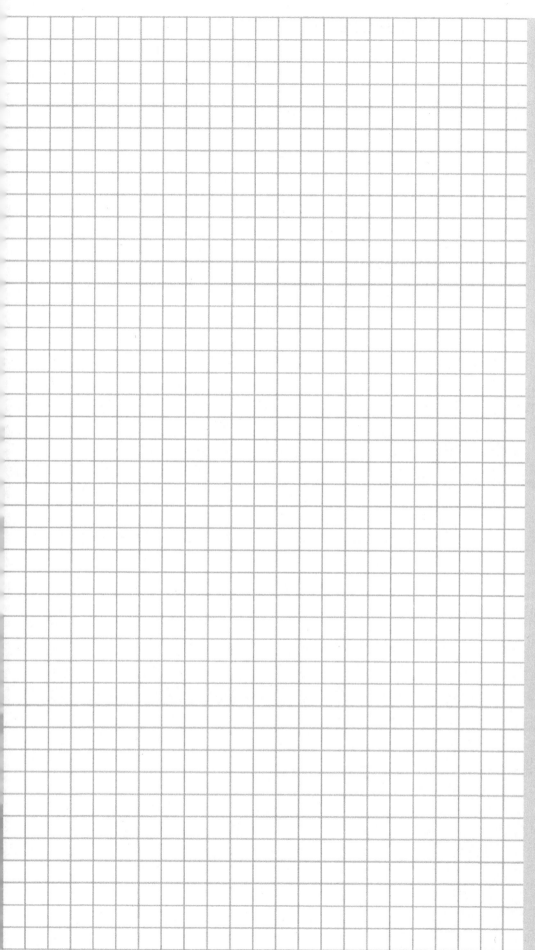

MEASUREMENTS

COLORS

TEXTURES

NOTES

NOTES

INDEX

REF #	PROJECT TITLE	PAGE

INDEX

REF #	PROJECT TITLE	PAGE

INDEX

REF #	PROJECT TITLE	PAGE

Made in United States
North Haven, CT
28 December 2024

63684399R00128